STEP-UP
GEOGRAPHY

Contrasting Localities

Ruth Nason & Julia Roche

Evans

Published by Evans Brothers Limited
2A Portman Mansions
Chiltern Street
London W1U 6NR

Reprinted 2008

© Evans Brothers Limited 2005

Produced for Evans Brothers Limited by
White-Thomson Publishing Ltd,
Bridgewater Business Centre,
210 High Street,
Lewes, East Sussex BN7 2NH

Printed in China by New Era Printing Co. Ltd.

Project manager: Ruth Nason

Designer: Helen Nelson, Jet the Dog

Consultant: John Lace, School Improvement
Manager, Hampshire County Council

Cover: All photographs by Chris Fairclough

British Library Cataloguing in Publication Data

Nason, Ruth
    Contrasting localities - (Step-up geography)
    1. Great Britain - Geography - Juvenile
    literature
    I. Title
    II. Roche, Julia

ISBN 978 0 237 528782

Picture acknowledgements:

Corbis: pages 4b (London Aerial Photo Library), 9b
(Hulton-Deutsch Collection), 10b (Macduff Everton),
11t (Ric Ergenbright), 12b (London Aerial Photo
Library), 15b (Gideon Mendel), 17b (Richard
Klune), 19 (Derek Croucher), 23t (Ric Ergenbright),
26b (Gideon Mendel); Mary Evans Picture Library:
pages 8, 9t; Chris Fairclough: pages 11br, 16, 20t,
20b, 24r; Chris Fairclough Photo Library: pages 4t,
5t, 5b, 10t, 11c, 11bl, 12t, 13, 14, 15t, 17t, 21,
24l, 27; HarperCollins Publishers: page 7; Topfoto:
pages 22, 23b, 26t (Universal Pictorial Press). The
painting of 'The Beach' by L. S. Lowry on page 25
is reproduced by courtesy of Felix Rosenstiel's
Widow & Son Ltd, London.

Maps and diagrams by Helen Nelson.

Contents

Localities

The photographs on these two pages show four different kinds of locality. Use an atlas to help you match the four places to the red dots on the map.

▶ Weymouth is a seaside town. Do you think it is busier in summer or in winter?

▼ This aerial view shows some of the city centre of Birmingham. The city grew big in the nineteenth century as a centre of industry and manufacturing.

The town of Croydon is a suburb of London. Suburbs are towns that are joined up with a larger town or city nearby.

Describing your locality

All these words describe types of locality. Which words describe the place where you live?

- City
- Commuter town
- Industrial town
- Port
- Rural town
- Seaside town
- Suburb
- Tourist centre
- Village

▲ *Where on this map do you live?*

Ae is a village in southwest Scotland. What do you think people would say are the advantages and disadvantages of living here?

On the map

What could you tell about a locality in the British Isles by looking at its location on a map like this? It shows physical features such as mountains and rivers.

Landscape

The map shows which are the main mountainous areas. Are they mainly in the north, south, east or west?

Which type of landscape do you like best, out of flat, hilly and mountainous? Why?

If there is water in your favourite landscape, what form does it take? Perhaps it is a fast-flowing stream, a wide river, a tranquil lake, or big, crashing waves at the coast.

Climate

The climate varies across the British Isles. On average, the south is warmer than the north, and the west is wetter than the east. Flat areas by the coast have the most sun in a year. In winter it is warmer by the coast than inland. In summer, inland is warmer than the coast.

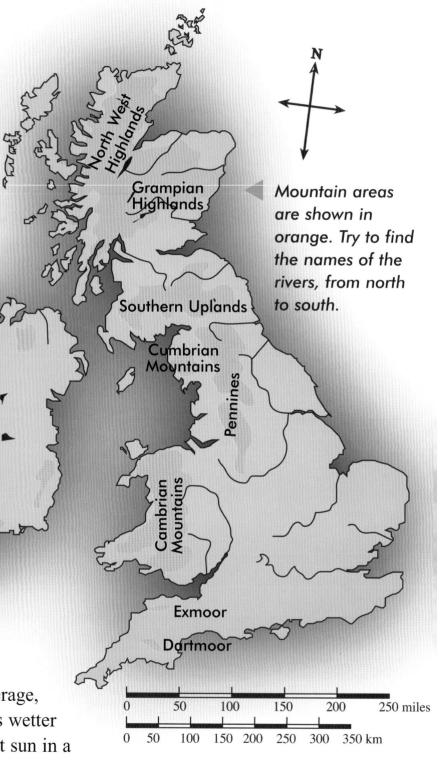

N

Mountain areas are shown in orange. Try to find the names of the rivers, from north to south.

North West Highlands

Grampian Highlands

Southern Uplands

Cumbrian Mountains

Pennines

Cambrian Mountains

Exmoor

Dartmoor

| 0 | 50 | 100 | 150 | 200 | 250 miles |

| 0 | 50 | 100 | 150 | 200 | 250 | 300 | 350 km |

Why is the west wetter?

Winds from the west blow weather depressions across the Atlantic Ocean and the British Isles. These depressions bring rain clouds. When they are blown up over the mountains, the water vapour in them cools and condenses and falls as rain.

The area to the east of the mountains is called the rain shadow. It is dry, since there is little moisture left in the air that blows across it.

Why are some places colder?

See if you can explain why the north is colder than the south. Think about the position of the British Isles in relation to the Equator.

Also see if you can think why urban places tend to be warmer than rural ones.

A class display

Collect photographs for a class display to show the variety of landscape and climate of the British Isles. You could arrange the photographs around a map, with coloured thread linking the pictures to the appropriate part of the map.

Road maps

A road map can show how big a place is and how it is linked to other localities. Towns and cities may be linked by motorways and other main roads, railway lines and air. Smaller places are reached by fewer, smaller roads.

▼ *How can you tell from this road map that Doncaster is the main town in the area? Use a road atlas to find out what the symbols and colours mean.*

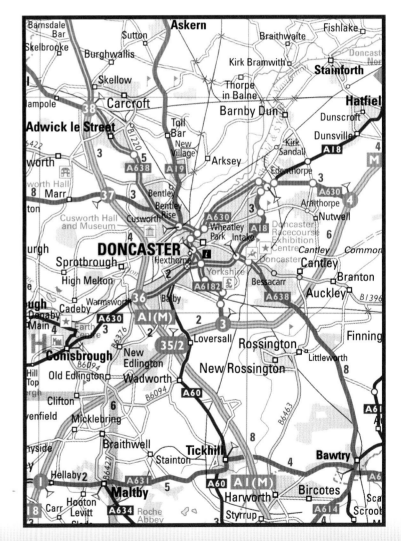

Where do places develop?

Some of the most important things that people need to survive are:

- water
- food
- a safe place to shelter
- materials to build shelters and make clothes
- a means of earning a living.

Villages and towns have started and grown up where people have found these things. For example, many places have grown up near a river.

Staying safe

Some places grew up around a fort or castle, which was built to defend the area against enemy attack.

On the coast, people settled by natural harbours where it was safe to moor their boats.

Some places developed as market towns, where people from nearby came to sell farm produce and goods they had made. Chichester is one example. This picture is from 1814.

Spa towns

It became fashionable to visit certain towns in order to drink and bathe in water from springs, called spas, discovered there. These towns grew, and transport routes to them improved, as the numbers of visitors increased.

The industrial revolution

Many towns grew large as industries developed in the nineteenth century. Manchester grew from a small market town into the world's biggest cotton-manufacturing city. Industrial towns needed transport links for bringing in raw materials and for trading the goods they produced. Many canals and railway lines were built at this time.

▶ *Why do you think many towns grew up near railway lines?*

▲ *Scarborough is a spa town by the sea. Visitors in the early nineteenth century believed the waters were good for their health. Later the town became popular for seaside holidays.*

Times and places change

Farmers no longer take their animals to market in Chichester. Manchester is no longer full of cotton factories. In many industrial cities, factory buildings have been changed into museums, shops or housing. Perhaps there are buildings that have changed use like this in your town.

Buildings

Like people, all localities have their own character. The landscape and the history of a place contribute to its character, and so do the buildings.

Tourist attractions

Some places are famous for having a special building such as a cathedral, a pier, a castle or a tower. A building like this attracts tourists to the town.

Tourists need somewhere to park, refreshment and, possibly, somewhere to stay. Can you think of anything else? What buildings would you therefore expect to find in a town that has many visitors?

▼ *Wells is the smallest city in Britain. The front of its cathedral is covered with stone carvings of about 300 saints and kings.*

▲ *Visitors to the Blackpool Tower can travel to the top in a lift, to see the view all around.*

Looking down

Find Blackpool, in Lancashire, and Wells, in Somerset, on a map of Britain. Then imagine looking down from the top of (a) Blackpool Tower and (b) one of the towers of Wells Cathedral. What differences and similarities would there be between the views?

Here is an example of houses built from local materials. The roofs are made from slate, taken from the slate mines in the background.

Building materials

In the past, houses were built with materials from nearby. For example, in Aberdeen, walls were built from granite. The grey, solid appearance of the buildings is a part of Aberdeen's character.

Bricks are made from clay, and the colour of clay varies around the British Isles. So bricks can be pale yellow, reddish, dark brown or black.

Today materials can be transported over long distances. What effect do you think this has on the materials people choose for building?

Building styles

Styles of building change over time. See if you can put the houses in these three pictures in order of their age. Which one do you most like the look of? Which would you most like to live in?

Town layouts

The picture at the bottom of this page is an aerial view of the centre of Milton Keynes. Many towns in Britain have grown gradually over hundreds of years, but Milton Keynes was built as a big new town about 30 years ago. The British government lent money for new towns to be built, because many older towns and cities were becoming overcrowded.

▲ This village has grown gradually. Its buildings are arranged in an irregular way.

◄ Compare this view of Milton Keynes with the one of Birmingham on page 4. What difference is there in the way the buildings are arranged?

The new towns were designed to be healthy places to live and work. They were also designed to be free of traffic problems. What evidence of this do you think there is in the photograph?

Town areas

Shops and offices are usually found in the centre of a town. Residential areas are clustered around the centre. Industrial areas tend to be on the outskirts of town.

New 'shopping centres' have also been built on the outskirts of some towns. Shoppers are attracted to them because they are easy to drive to, have large car parks and may charge cheaper prices. However, some people are worried that town centres will lose their lively atmosphere if shoppers are attracted away from them. What do you think?

Green areas

Areas of grass and trees are important parts of towns and cities. They are places where people can get away from traffic noise and fumes. Trees also help to keep the air clean, as they take in carbon dioxide and give out oxygen. Carbon dioxide is one of the gases in traffic fumes which harm our environment.

Another important green area is the green belt. A green belt is an area of countryside around a town where new building is not allowed.

A green survey

Do a class survey about places in your locality where you go for fresh air and exercise: for example, parks or playing fields. How far from people's homes are these places? How do they travel there? What changes would you like to make to improve these areas?

▲ *The character of a town is influenced by its layout and its green areas are an important part of this.*

Populations

Like many towns, Milton Keynes (see page 12) has a website: www.mkweb.co.uk. It tells us that 50 per cent of commuters in Milton Keynes travel less than three miles to work. Commuters are people who travel between their home and work every weekday.

You could do a survey to find out about commuters where you live. How far do the parents or guardians of children in your class travel to work? Work out percentages of people who travel different distances, such as 'under 5 miles', 'between 5 and 10 miles', and so on.

▲ *These people are on their way home from work in London.*

Commuter towns

Commuter towns have grown up around cities, for people who work in the city but want to live somewhere quieter. Many commuter towns are linked to the city by a railway line, so it is convenient for people to travel to work by train. Houses in a commuter town are often expensive, because the city workers who want to live there with their families can afford high prices.

Try listing some differences you think there may be between commuter towns and other towns. At what times of day and of the week would a commuter town be busiest?

Younger or older?

The Milton Keynes website says that 46 per cent of its population are under 30 years old. This is a higher percentage of young people than in most other towns. Some rural and seaside towns have a larger proportion of older people, who have retired from work.

How do you think the age of the population affects the character of a town?

◀ *Some people move to a new locality after they retire from work. Many choose a place on the south coast of England. Why do you think this might suit some older people?*

Newcomers

Many people move to a place because there is work for them there. Moving can be exciting, but also hard as it takes time to feel 'at home' in a new place.

A large city is influenced by all the people who move into it from around the world. They help to give it a cosmopolitan character.

A welcome pack

What information do you think it would be helpful to give to a family moving in to your locality? Put together a pack of information to help newcomers feel 'at home'. What else could you do to welcome new residents?

▲ *In some places newcomers arrive from other countries. Families from Asia have moved to towns around the British Isles, including some of the big cities that grew up because of their industries.*

Caring for a locality

Local councils are responsible for looking after villages, towns and cities. Local people pay a council tax and the council decides how to use this money to keep the locality safe and pleasant for everyone.

There are many things to share the money between, including:

- repairing roads and building new ones
- improving road systems, for example with one-way streets, new roundabouts, disabled parking spaces, and pedestrianised areas
- putting in new lighting and security cameras
- collecting rubbish
- looking after green areas.

Local concerns

Look in the 'Letters' pages in your local newspapers. You will probably find letters from people expressing their worries about the way the town is being looked after, or about changes that are happening there. Do you agree with their concerns?

When you visit a locality, what signs do you think tell you whether it is well cared for?

▶ *In many localities you will see signs of schemes to encourage people to recycle their rubbish. Local councils are trying to increase the proportion of household rubbish that is recycled.*

Town planning

One department of the local council must look at plans for new buildings and give their approval before building work begins. They consider whether the building is 'in keeping' with the character of the locality. This includes looking at its proposed size and style and the materials it would be built from.

Regeneration

The industries that grew up in the nineteenth century helped Britain to become a wealthy country with a high standard of living. But eventually the industries declined. People were left unemployed and factory areas became wasteland in the middle of the city.

▲ This new building work is happening on a brownfield site, which has been used for building before. This is preferable to using 'new' land.

Happily, many of these areas have been brought to life again. The docks by the canal in Salford are one example. The canal and docks were built for sea-going ships that travelled up the River Mersey to the Salford factories. When the factories closed, the area became deserted. But now it has been regenerated with exciting new buildings.

◀ The rebuilt Salford Docks area includes an arts centre called the Lowry. See if you can find out who it was named after.

Preparing for a field trip

If you are going on a field trip to investigate a locality, you will need to plan your route. It's also good to find out about the place before you go, so that you know the interesting things to look out for.

If you are not going on a field trip at the moment, you could plan a journey to a place that you would like to visit one day. Choose somewhere very different from your own locality. You might like to consider Winchester, Leeds, Colchester, Stoke-on-Trent, Blackpool or Liverpool.

Where it is

Find your destination in a road atlas. Then use one of the eight points of the compass to describe its direction from you, 'as the crow flies'.

▼ Many road atlases include a chart like this, showing distances between places. Use this chart or one from a road atlas to work out the distance from your school to the place you are going to visit. You may need to find the distance from your nearest large town and then add the extra distance between that town and school.

Journey planner

Visit http://www.transport-direct.info/TransportDirect/en. You can research your journey by car and by public transport. How long would it take to get there by train? How many times would you need to change train?

Birmingham	Blackpool	Colchester	Leeds	Liverpool	Stoke-on-Trent	Winchester	London
130							
171	296						
121	87	199					
102	59	264	74				
48	86	212	93	57			
121	257	147	226	228	176		
120	243	62	198	215	162	66	

Conwy is on the coast of North Wales. As well as the castle, it has other buildings to visit from medieval, Elizabethan and Victorian times. You can also walk along the top of the walls which surround the oldest part of the town.

Places of interest

Find out about places of special interest in the locality you are going to, such as museums, castles or historic houses, working factories or historic dockyards. You could write to the local Tourist Information Office and request leaflets about things to do and see. Or find their website by going to http://www.tourist-information-uk.com/tourist-offices-uk.htm.

Industrial history

Find out if the locality became famous for a particular industry or economic activity and, if so, why this happened. The local history society will have information about this. Go to http://www.local-history.co.uk/Groups. Select the appropriate county for your locality and follow the links.

How will it be different?

Make a list of the differences you expect to notice between the place you are going to and the place where you live. Think about:

- the landscape
- the weather
- the style of buildings
- shops and businesses
- the people, their work and leisure interests
- roads and traffic.

What could you investigate?

On your journey to visit a locality, make a note of what you see, especially as you get closer to your destination.

- What kind of homes do you notice: high-rise flats, detached, semi-detached or terraced houses, bungalows?

- What is growing in the fields?

- Are there cattle, sheep or pigs?

- Are there factories? If so, what clues are there about what is being made?

Physical features and land use

One good way to start to learn about a place is to go to a good viewpoint, for example the highest hill or the top of a tall building. Draw a set of four or five pictures of what you can see, looking in different directions.

▲ *As well as sketching views, you could take photographs.*

◄ *An advantage of sketching is that it makes you look very carefully at what you see.*

Use a compass so you can label your pictures like this: 'View looking northeast from ....' (add the name of the hill or building).

While you look at the view, also make some quick notes about:

- what the land is used for (e.g. arable or dairy farming, leisure, housing)

- any special landmarks (e.g. windmill, church with tower or spire, farm, railway line)

- people and what they are doing (e.g. harvesting, building, playing a sport).

Land use in the main street

Walk along the main street and notice what types of shops and other buildings there are. You could make a simple plan of the street and any side streets. Then mark on the different types of building. Beforehand, devise a key for the different types, such as banks, charity shops, card shops, food shops, cafés and restaurants, chemists, estate agents.

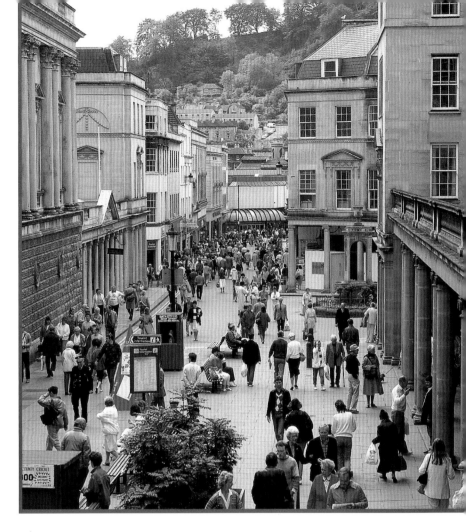

▲ *What notes might you make as you looked at this view in Bath?*

Tally charts

After your field trip, use your completed street plan to make a tally chart of your findings. Then use the data and a computer to make a block graph. You could carry out the same survey in your own high street and compare your findings.

▼ *What title would you give your graph?*

Banks	Cafés	Charity shops	Estate agents	Chemists	Card shops	Food shops

Finding out what people do

Your investigations of land use (pages 20-21) will give you clues about what people in the locality do, for work and in their leisure time.

What people do in a locality is influenced by:

- its location, e.g. inland or on the coast
- the presence of a particular commodity, e.g. coal, clay, or fish
- its position in relation to roads, railway lines, ports and airports
- its links to historical events, e.g. battles or invasions.

Which of these influences do you think is strongest in the locality you are investigating?

People and the environment

Over time the work that people do affects the environment. That is easy to see in a town like St Austell in Cornwall, which developed because of the presence of china clay. The clay is mined from rocks and processed. Land is taken over for quarrying, buildings and transport links. More people have moved to the area because there is work for them, and so the town has grown to house them and their families.

◀ *The china clay industry has changed the landscape near St Austell.*

The county of Kent was known for growing hops, which are used in making beer. The hops were dried in buildings with a cone-shaped roof, called oast houses. Today many oast houses have been turned into homes.

What other examples can you think of where the work people do affects the environment?

Types of work

Ask this series of questions about the locality you are investigating:

- Is this area known as a source for one particular commodity?

- If yes, what is it? (E.g. fish from sea fishing.)

- If no, is the area known for making a particular product?

- If yes, what is it? (E.g. paper.)

- If no, what are the main ways in which people in the area make a living? (E.g. tourism.)

Llandudno on the north coast of Wales developed as a holiday resort. What type of work do you think people do here?

What does it feel like?

There are many ways in which we can enjoy and appreciate the atmosphere of a locality. We develop a feel for a place through our senses of sight, hearing and smell.

▲ Try to notice shapes and textures.

◄ Have you been to a place where you saw reflections in water?

Poets, composers and artists

Poets, composers and artists have created works about places which have stirred their emotions. Try reading some of the poems listed on the right and make notes about things in them that you like. You can find all the poems at www.poemhunter.com.

- 'Sea Fever' by John Masefield
- 'My Heart's in the Highlands' by Robert Burns
- 'From a Railway Carriage' by Robert Louis Stevenson
- 'A Bay in Anglesey' by John Betjeman
- 'Composed upon Westminster Bridge' by William Wordsworth.

▲ *This is a painting called 'The Beach' by the English artist L. S. Lowry. How many colours can you count in the sand?*

Your location, your feelings

On page 20 it was suggested that you go to a viewpoint and make sketches. Perhaps you could also just sit quietly there, away from your friends but still in view of your group leader, and do nothing except use your senses of sight, hearing and smell.

Try to see and hear things that you might not normally notice with lots of noise going on. You might hear bees, the swish of grasses in the breeze, the sound of a stream trickling over stones or even your own breathing. You might be able to smell the sea or wild flowers.

Try to remember what you have seen and sensed and, after your quiet time, jot down some words and phrases to remind you later.

Be a poet

Use the sketches and jottings you made at the viewpoint to help you compose a poem. Try to use lots of adverbs and adjectives and also some alliteration, similes **and** metaphors.

How will places change?

What examples can you remember from earlier in this book of places changing over time? Places change because:

- people move in or away
- patterns of work change
- new technology is invented
- people's ideas and tastes alter.

The twenty-first century

How do you think localities will change as a result of things that are happening now, in the early twenty-first century? For example, think about the effects of:

- increasing use of internet shopping
- the need to reduce air pollution
- increasing contact and cooperation with other countries.

▶ *Findhorn Ecovillage in Scotland has been built to show how people can live without harming the environment. For example, they use local materials for building and grow their own food. By not using goods that are transported from far away, they are not adding to the air pollution caused by vehicles.*

▲ *More localities will probably try to introduce trams for public transport, as these are more environmentally friendly than buses. This would change the look, sound and smell of the town centre.*

Problems on the coast

Places on the coast are facing particular problems. Fewer people go on holiday to British seaside resorts, so local businesses connected with tourism are making less money. They cannot afford to employ so many local people. Some businesses close down.

People who make their living from sea fishing must follow new laws about how many fish they can catch. This is to prevent certain types of fish from dying out. However, the law makes it hard for sea-fishing businesses to make enough money to keep going.

How do you think these problems will change localities on the coast?

Scrapbook

Keep a scrapbook of cuttings from newspapers about changes that are happening in different places and the resulting improvements or problems.

Are places 'all the same'?

In this book we have looked at differences between localities. But some people say that town centres have become 'all the same' because so many shops are now branches of the same big chain stores. The shops in different places have the same names and fronts and so places lose their individual characters. Do you agree with this view?

▼ *Architects* **help to change our localities with the buildings they design. This is the office of the mayor in London. Would a building like this look good in your locality?**

Glossary

aerial view a view from the air, looking down.

alliteration using words next to each other which begin with the same sound.

arable farming growing crops rather than keeping animals.

architect someone qualified to design buildings and supervise their construction.

brownfield site a site for new building, which has had buildings on it in the past.

canal a manmade water course. Many canals were used as transport links between industrial localities.

cathedral the main church building in a district called a diocese, which is overseen by a bishop.

chain stores shops which have branches in many different places.

character all the qualities of someone or something, which make the person or thing unique.

china clay a fine white clay used in making thin white china and in making paper.

city a town with a cathedral, or an important large town.

climate the average weather of a place over a period of time.

coast the line or area where the land meets the sea or a lake.

commodity a substance, material or foodstuff that can be traded.

commuter someone who travels each day between work and home.

condense turn from a gas into a liquid.

cosmopolitan representing all parts of the world.

council the group of people who are elected to run a town or village.

council tax money paid by each household in a town or village to their local council. It is used by the council to pay for local services such as libraries, street cleaning and school crossing patrols.

county one of the many parts into which the UK is divided, e.g. Cornwall, Cumbria, Dyfed, Norfolk, Berkshire.

dairy farming rearing cattle, mainly to produce milk, butter and cheese.

depression low air pressure, bringing bad weather.

destination the place to which you are going.

docks a manmade area of water for cargo ships to stop and load or unload.

economic activity an activity designed to make money.

environment the surroundings in which people, plants and animals live.

environmentally friendly designed to be good for the environment or not to damage it.

Equator an imaginary line around the centre of the Earth. Every point on this line is equally distant from the north and south poles.

field trip	a visit to a site, to investigate a real example of something you are learning about.
granite	a hard grey rock.
green belt	open land surrounding a town.
harbour	a shelter for ships.
inland	away from the coast.
leisure	free time used for having fun.
locality	a place.
location	where something is.
metaphor	a way of describing something by using a word for something else, which it is like. E.g. 'Sparkling, pretty things were a *magnet* for her.' (This means they attracted her.)
motorway	a road for fast-moving traffic. Motorways have more lanes than other main roads and fewer junctions where traffic can join or leave them.
new town	a town planned and built to prevent existing towns and cities from becoming overcrowded.
outskirts	areas of a town or village away from the centre.
physical features	the natural parts that make up the Earth's surface, e.g. mountains, rivers and seas.
pier	a long structure which sticks out from the land into the sea. People can walk along it and boats can land at it.
port	a town with a harbour, which has developed as a landing place.

quarrying	digging a material from an open mine.
rain shadow	an area to one side of mountains, away from where the wind blows, where less than average rain falls.
raw materials	natural materials used in the process of making something.
regenerated	rebuilt or renewed.
residential area	part of a town where people live.
retired	no longer going to work.
route	the way to go in order to arrive at a particular place.
rural	in the countryside.
simile	a description of something that likens it to something else. E.g. 'The cake was as light as a feather.'
spa	a spring, where the water that bubbles out of the ground contains mineral substances.
suburb	a town which has become a district of a larger town or city, as both have spread and joined together.
tally chart	a chart used to count the numbers of certain things.
urban	belonging to a town or city.
village	a group of houses and other buildings, smaller than a town, and usually in the country.
wasteland	a deserted, uncared-for area.
water vapour	gas formed when water evaporates.

For teachers and parents

This book is designed to support the teaching of Unit 13 of the QCA Geography Scheme of Work.

In investigating the physical features and human factors which make places different from each other, children will have opportunities to develop their skills in:

- locating places on maps;
- using atlases and maps;
- using secondary sources;
- using geographical vocabulary;
- using ICT to access information;
- undertaking fieldwork;
- making maps and plans;
- collecting and recording evidence;
- analysing and communicating;
- appreciating the quality of an environment;
- communicating and explaining issues.

Many cross-curricular links can also be made, to Literacy (especially speaking and listening), Maths, History, Art, ICT, Drama, Citizenship and PSHE.

If you can find a copy of *Mouldy's Orphan* by Gillian Avery (Puffin Books, 1981), it might be good to read as a serialised story while you are doing this unit. It is set in Victorian times and would be a useful point of reference for some of the historical research to be undertaken.

SUGGESTED FURTHER ACTIVITIES

Pages 4-5 Localities

These pages present a good opportunity for some work on maps and latitude/longitude co-ordinates. Two school atlases with some helpful information on this are *The New Oxford School Atlas* (ISBN 0-19-831667-4) and *Philip's Modern School Atlas* (ISBN 0540080888). After doing some preparatory work, the children could use their own classroom atlases to find and record the co-ordinates of the four places indicated by red dots on the map.

You might like to discuss and record the children's views on the advantages and disadvantages of living where they do. Each child could then be invited to suggest one thing that could be done to improve the locality. The suggestions could form part of a display.

Pages 6-7 On the map

As a follow-up to the activities on pages 6-7 you could make a link between the system of road communications left by the Romans and the road system now. Discuss the reasons for the Roman pattern.

http://www.schoolhistory.co.uk/year7links/romans/romanroads.pdf has an excellent activity which involves using atlases to find the Roman towns named and then joining groups of them to show eleven important Roman roads.

Pages 8-9 Where do places develop?

Some interesting local history work could arise from the end of this section. With the help of your public library, your local history society and interviews with older residents and relatives, the children could research any major changes in the use of local buildings. E.g.

- The old school is now used by a local organ builder or by a firm of architects, as offices.
- An old church has been converted into a family home.
- A baker's shop and restaurant became a book shop and now a charity shop.

You might also invite someone from your local history society to come in and talk to the children about the development of your locality.

Pages 10-11 Buildings

For some panoramic views of places around the British Isles, children could visit http://www.bbc.co.uk/england/webcams and click on the county they are researching.

To extend the work on page 11, the children could produce a drawing of the exterior of their home. Then, perhaps with some help from an adult, they could label the different features on the drawing (e.g. bricks, roof tiles, gutters, down pipes, windows, doors) and discuss the materials used. Later, in class, you might discuss whether or not any of the materials used are local, such as Cotswold stone or Welsh slate. Your local builder's merchant might be able to help here.

Pages 12-13 Town layouts

There are some schemes which encourage the planting of trees to enhance the environment for future generations. Visit http://www.treeforall.org.uk to find out about the many things that are happening all over the country but especially in your own area. This is an attractive, user-friendly site and, at the time of writing, they are offering free tree packs and complimentary educational resources and planting instructions. The children would love to feel that they are 'doing their bit' for the environment.

Pages 14-15 Populations

In many localities there is concern at government proposals for building new homes. Nobody disagrees that many more affordable homes are needed. The concern arises because the plans are for the new homes to be built in already densely populated areas, possibly using some greenfield sites. Discuss with the children the terms 'brownfield' and 'greenfield' and then discuss the strain that additional homes and numbers of people would put on the existing infrastructure, e.g. schools and roads. Ask the children to add their own ideas.

Some Maths work could be built in here, by researching the population growth of your town during the last century. You might try to find figures from 1900, 1910, 1920 etc. up to and including 2000 and make graphs to show your findings.

Pages 16-17 Caring for a locality

From looking at letters in your local newspapers, the children will perhaps be aware of some of the issues that are troubling people in your locality. List some of their findings on the board and discuss which ones they most identify with.

Remind the children of some of the conventions of letter writing and show some examples of well-written letters which you have collected. Help the children to see that the letters you have chosen are polite and to the point and that all the arguments made are clear and concise. Now ask the children to choose an issue and write their own letter to an imaginary editor. Use a word processing package if possible.

Pages 18-19 Planning a visit

This would be a good opportunity to take the children to your local public library, as many of them may not have been there before. It is best to give the library notice of your visit well in advance and tell them about the information the children will be looking for, so that they can ensure that they are well stocked on that particular topic. It is useful for the children to have been taught how libraries work. You could build on what is known already by those who do use the library, and you may have the Dewey system in place in your own school library. The librarians will, almost certainly, have other activities to suggest, so that you can divide the class into groups or even take half the class one day and half on another occasion.

Pages 20-21 Investigating a locality

As part of a display you might work with the children to make a long collage picture of your visited high street. The children could use photographs taken on the field trip to help them make drawings of specific buildings, all at a given size (e.g. to fill a given sheet of paper). The drawings could then be cut out and mounted in order, perhaps with one side of the street above the other side.

Pages 22-23 Finding out what people do

During your visit you could arrange for the children to carry out a traffic survey. Try to visit the site of your survey at a time when there is little traffic and again when it is very busy. You can then use the children's findings to stimulate discussion.

Back in the classroom spend some time discussing how the children will record and present their data. You might also discuss:

- the impact of the volume of traffic on the environment, looking at issues such as ease of movement and safety of pedestrians;

- the effects of traffic on air pollution;

- why the roads are busier at some times more than others.

The discussion could also focus on what the land is used for and what people do here.

http://www.schoolshistory.org.uk/IndustrialRevolution contains useful background information, as does http://www.bbc.co.uk/history/forkids, which has an Anglo-Saxon link giving some place-name suffixes which the children might find interesting.

Pages 24-25 What does it feel like?

You might want to follow up some of the work here by building on the children's knowledge of colour mixing. Then encourage them to turn some of their drawings into paintings, using varying shades of colour as, for example, Lowry did.

Some children might like to do weaving on small, forked twigs, using a variety of coloured wools (brought from home) to represent the overall colours of the place they observed.

Pages 26-27 How will places change?

There is a very nice site about seaside holidays now and in the past at: www.eadt.co.uk/eduzone/seaside/content/Now%20and%20Then/link_par_gp.asp.

Some useful research and data collection could be done in your class or in several classes, about holiday destinations now and in the past. Using computers, the children could compose a questionnaire with numbered questions, requiring only yes or no answers. E.g.
1) Do you take your holidays in the UK?
2) Do you take your holidays abroad?
3) 4) 5) 6) 7) Do you travel by car, coach, train, ferry, plane?
Some interesting Maths work could be done, turning the responses into graphs and percentages.

Index